W9-BZW-552

EARTH'S SEASONS & CYCLES

Reviewed by Mark Sisson,
Principal Engineer,
The Boeing Company

Christine Dugan

Table of Contents

Changes on Earth

Have you ever wondered why summer has to end and autumn begins? Do you ever wonder why it rains and snows? Do you ever wish that nighttime would never come so you can play in the daylight forever? Have you ever looked at the moon and wondered why it's bright and full one night and doesn't seem to be there on another?

There are answers for all these questions, and they all have to do with changes on Earth.

3

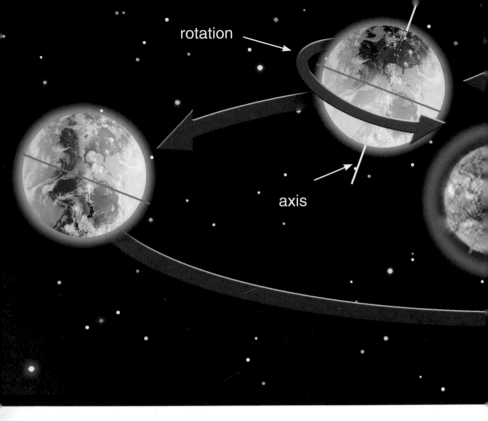

rotation

axis

Some changes on Earth happen again and again. We call these *cycles*. Some of these cycles are caused by the way Earth moves around the sun.

A **cycle** (SI-kəl) is a series of events that happen again and again, in the same order.

orbit

Rotation and Revolution

Earth moves in two ways. They are called *rotation* and *revolution*. To rotate means to spin on an *axis*. To revolve means to *orbit*.

So, Earth rotates on its axis while it revolves, or orbits, around the sun.

- An **axis** (AK-sǝs) is an imaginary line down the center. Earth's axis goes from north to south.

- To **orbit** means to move in a circle or oval around something else.

5

Earth's Cycle of Seasons

Earth's spinning causes a cycle of changing *seasons*. There are four seasons each year: spring, summer, autumn, and winter. The seasons are not the same everywhere at the same time. They are different because of Earth's rotations and revolutions.

Here is how it works.

Earth rotates one time each day. But Earth's axis is not straight up and down. It tilts a little. So, Earth tilts a little, too.

Earth orbits or circles the sun one time each year. That makes one revolution.

Since Earth is tilted, the sun's most direct rays strike Earth at different places depending on Earth's rotation and revolution. Some places experience daylight while other places experience nighttime. This is a result of the Earth's rotations and revolutions.

Leap Year

One revolution takes 365 days and 6 hours. What happens to those extra hours? Every four years, we add a day to the end of February, creating a leap year. This extra day makes our calendar match with Earth's revolutions.

Spring

Summer

Winter

Autumn

▲ Earth is always on the move. We may not feel it, but there are signs of Earth's motion all around us. Changing seasons are one important sign.

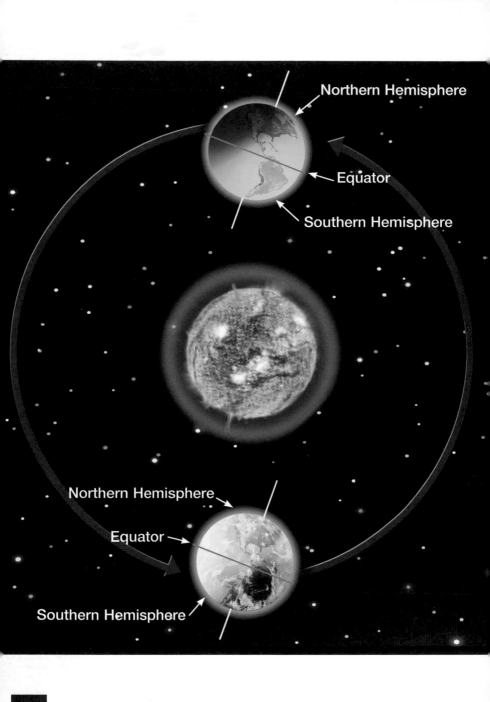

Northern Hemisphere

Equator

Southern Hemisphere

Northern Hemisphere

Equator

Southern Hemisphere

Earth is divided by the *equator*. Everything north of the equator is the *northern hemisphere*. Everything south of it is the *southern hemisphere*.

When the northern hemisphere is tilted away from the sun, it is autumn and winter there. At the same time, the southern hemisphere is tilted toward the sun. It is spring and summer there. So, in January while people in the United States are experiencing the cold of winter, people in South America are feeling the warmth of summer.

Changing Seasons

When Earth moves to the other side of the sun, half way through the year, the seasons switch in the northern and southern hemispheres.

The **equator** (i-KWAT-er) is an imaginary line that wraps around the middle of Earth, from east to west and back again.

The **solstice** (sol-stis) is the time of year when the sun reaches the farthest north or the farthest south, making the longest and shortest days of the year.

Have you noticed that days are longer in summer and shorter in winter? The longest day in the summer is called the summer *solstice*. The shortest day in the winter is called the winter solstice. When a hemisphere tilts toward the sun, it gets more sunlight through the day than when it tilts away from the sun.

Think about people who live far north and south. In winter, they may not see the sun at all or only very briefly. But in summer, they may see it almost all the time! Imagine that!

There are also days each year when day and night are equal lengths. The autumnal *equinox* and the vernal equinox are the two days when day and night last 12 hours each. The autumnal equinox is the first day of autumn in the northern hemisphere and the

6:00 a.m.

first day of spring in the southern hemisphere. The vernal equinox is the first day of autumn in the southern hemisphere and the first day of spring in the northern hemisphere.

The **equinox** (eh-KWA-nox) is a time when night and day are of equal length in all parts of the Earth.

6:00 p.m.

▲ There are only two days each year when daylight and darkness are the same length of time.

Day and Night

Remember that Earth rotates once each day. So, a point on Earth faces the sun for just a part of the day. The rest of the time it rotates away from the sun.

▲ The only real difference between ▶ day and night is that during the night, natural light and the heat that goes with it disappear until the morning.

As it rotates away, daylight becomes night. As it rotates back, night becomes morning. Round and round Earth goes, turning day to night and back again.

Did you know?
When it is daylight for you, it is night on the other side of the world.

Moon Phases

While Earth rotates and revolves around the sun, the moon rotates and revolves around Earth.

As the moon moves, sometimes it is between Earth and the sun. Sometimes it is behind Earth, and sometimes it is to the side.

The moon's place makes a difference. The moon does not make its own light. It lights up because it reflects light from the sun. Because of this, the moon seems to grow through the month from blackness to fullness and back again. During a full moon, the sun lights the entire face of the moon. During a new moon, the moon is between the sun and Earth. The sun lights the side away from Earth, so we cannot see it. There are also nights when we can only see parts of the moon.

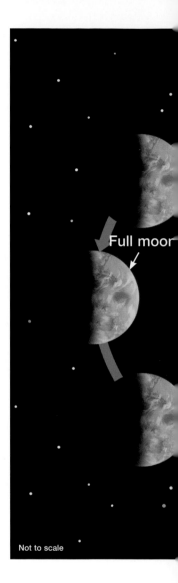

Full moon

Not to scale

New moon

▲ How Long?

The moon's rotation and revolution are the same length of time, about 27 days (or about one month).

Tides

Moon and Earth are pulled toward each other by *gravity*. Moon's pull on Earth causes the oceans to be pulled toward the moon. The oceans facing the moon bulge out, and we call this *high tide*.

The other side of Earth has a high tide then, too, because the land is being pulled toward the moon and away from the water. So, the water appears to rise higher.

Because of the ways the moon and Earth move, each ocean shore has a high tide and *low tide* about twice each day.

Gravity is a natural force that causes objects to be pulled toward each other. On Earth, we experience this as the force that holds us onto the planet.

High tide happens when ocean water comes higher and farther onto the shore. **Low tide** is when it rolls further away from the shore.

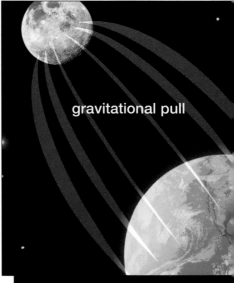

gravitational pull

▲ The ocean tides on Earth are caused by the gravitational pull between Earth and the moon.

▲ High tide in the Bay of Fundy

When Earth, the sun, and the moon are all in a line, their gravity works together on the tides. These are called *spring tides*. Spring tides are especially strong, or high. They don't just happen during the spring season, however.

▲ Low tide in the Bay of Fundy

Neap tides are very weak, or low, tides. They happen whenever Earth and the sun and moon are opposite of each other.

Water Cycle

The sun causes another cycle on Earth. Earth has a limited amount of water. The water always moves and changes during what is called the *water cycle*. Water from Earth's surface, such as in our oceans and lakes, is heated by the sun. The sun changes the water from liquid to gas. This process is called *evaporation*.

Next, water forms tiny droplets in clouds. This process is called *condensation*. When those clouds and cool air are mixed, certain kinds of weather such as rain and snow are formed. This weather, called *precipitation*, causes water to return to Earth's surface.

- **Evaporation** (i-VAP-o-rā-shun) is the process in which water changes from a liquid to a gas.
- **Condensation** (con-den-SA-shun) is the process in which water changes from a gas to a liquid.
- **Precipitation** (pri-sip-i-TA-shun) is water that falls from the sky as rain, snow, sleet, or hail.

condensation

evaporation

precipitation

When water falls from the sky, most of it runs off the land. It flows down hills and mountains. The water travels to streams, ponds, rivers, and lakes. It eventually returns to the oceans and seas.

Then, the water cycle starts all over again.

Water comes to Earth in many forms, such as rain, snow, sleet, and hail.

▲ Hail

▲ Rain

How Much Water?

How much water is there on Earth? Including both fresh and saltwater, there are about 326,000,000,000,000,000,000 gallons. (That means 326 million trillion!)

▲ Sleet

▲ Snow

Today's Earth

Think about where you live. What are seasons and cycles like in your town? Do you enjoy long summer days? What do you do on a cold winter's day?

Now, think about other places around the world. What is happening there while you are enjoying the sunshine, watching a full moon, or playing in the snow?

Earth's seasons and cycles are constantly changing. Each day and time is different in places all around the world. So, the next time you wake up to begin your day, think about a boy or girl on the other side of the world—and say, "Good night!"

Glossary

axis an imaginary line down the center

condensation the process by which a gas or vapor changes to a liquid

cycle a series of events that happen again and again, in the same order

equator the imaginary line that wraps around the middle of Earth

equinox one of two times during the year when day and night are of equal lengths

evaporation the process by which a liquid changes to a gas or vapor

gravity a natural force that causes objects to be pulled toward each other

high tide the time when the ocean is highest on the shore

low tide the time when the ocean is furthest back from the shore

moon phases cycles of the moon from full to new and back again

neap tide a weak tide

northern hemisphere on Earth, everything north of the equator

orbit move in a circle or oval shape around an object

precipitation weather—such as rain, snow, sleet, or hail—that falls from the sky

revolution one full orbit

rotation one full turn on an axis

seasons cycles of the Earth that are changed by Earth's placement around the sun

solstice when the sun reaches the farthest north or the farthest south, making the longest and shortest days of the year

southern hemisphere on Earth, everything south of the equator

spring tide an especially strong tide that occurs when Earth, the sun and the moon are all in line

water cycle movement of water on Earth from ocean, to sky, to land, and back to ocean

Index